Outside In

by

Polly Bull

First edition.

Cover artwork by Joey O'Gorman

Published by Wordville
London
2021
info@wordville.net

ISBN: 978-1-8384036-0-7

Acknowledgements

With thanks to Joanna Ingham and City Lit for guidance, Joey O'Gorman for artwork, to everyone at Celine's Salon, Speakeasy, Poetry LGBT, the Cheerfuls and Misericordia for listening and feedback, and to family and friends for loving support.

Special thanks to Leah for empowering me as a poet and person.

And eternal gratitude to Lucy, who has made this all possible.

In memory of my dad, Andy Bull (1955-2015).

Polly Bull

Polly is a poet, writer and content designer living, working and loving in London. Polly has a PhD in the history of reading and gender from the University of London. A regular at poetry nights such as Celine's Salon, Poetry LGBT and Speakeasy, their poetry draws on family memory, loss and personal and collective growth.

Contents

Cheese course

Dad was the high priest of the cheese course.
Supplies stocked up from Trader Joe's upon my prodigal returns from uni/LA/London:
a fine Cheddar (not American orange), the pale one, somewhat crystalline;
or a veiny, incorrigible Stilton.
Brie had to be triple cream.
Room temperature for eating, all were awakened from the fridge before the meal,
the holy communion of dairy and Port.
Accoutrements thus: a guillotine marble board; a homemade wooden chequered slab; a dainty knife, prongs and a razor edge.
The hardware varied over the years, but never the intention.
Inimitable, Dad's flamboyance emerged when divvying up the manna.
"Polly? A bit more Gouda?", with one delicate hand held open, encouraging, the other with the utensil pointing precisely at the sacrament.

There was no cheese that first trip back after the funeral.
We'd all become atheists anyway.

They are Magnolia Trees

'Look at the blossoms. They are Magnolia trees.'
'Pretty,' I reply to my mother.
We are doing our regular walk to the hospital.

We take the unpopulated route by the river and seagulls.
Broken down ghost boats, disintegrated like my synapses.
My brain has failed. Again.

The river winds inevitably into a basin, under a bridge.
'This is the canal to Birmingham.'
'Oh, I see,' I respond with difficulty, having forgotten
Birmingham.

We come to the garden centre at Syon House with the lion
statue.
I'm told I've been here before on a sunny picnic.
I cannot recall that picnic on this walk.

I'm wearing dilapidated black leather boots with 'Made in Spain',
written on the soles.
Letters scuffed away (I notice on the ward), now the left one
reads: 'pain'.
This is the only part that makes sense.

After the habitual fraught exchange at the hospital, we begin our
journey back.
'Look at the blossoms,' Mother says.
'Pretty,' I say.
'They are Magnolia trees.'

Lost smugglers

We are high tide at dusk,
and the menacing is becoming real.
In the vanished sunshine, waves beat down the walls of the crumbling mill at Lee Bay.
The beacon is lost in the gravy sky.
Our minds have fled as we stumble over tide pools, trying to get away.
Upon the cliffs we can't see the stinging nettles that punish our legs.
We feel nothing of the past, or the scent of the wet earth slippery beneath our uneven stride.
The old bruises that wound around our throats have faded, but the gallows beckon.
This smugglers' path is pointless.
It will be forgotten like everything else.
We thought the moon would guide us,
but it is just a fickle rock.

Hidden armour

We are sitting in the base of the turret,
mold in our noses as we inhale cold air, the breath of a thousand years.
The 15inch by 18inch television on a rolling stand lights up.
I sit ready, the child between Granny and Grandpa, adorned in 80s action wear, a life preserver red jacket, durable trousers and Velcro shoes.
On screen, a knight puts on his armour, more robot than man.
Crackling narration impresses us with numbers: 110lbs of shimmering metal.
A page boy assists and there is an order for putting it all on, a process.
The breastplate is one of the last silver puzzle pieces to be fastened tight with steadfast latches.

Today I am sitting on my bed, swiping through Instagram.
Reassured by a screen of affirmed enby folk, I open the package that has just been delivered.
The fabric is light, streamlined, well-made, metallic grey, certain.
Squeezing into it, I chuckle to myself: 'well, it's a bit tight,' as if a tree trunk is a bit wooden.
No need for a page boy, the binder immediately flattens my chest and I am exhilarated.
Confident. Comfortable.
Pulling on a tight T-shirt I can finally read the words that are no longer stretched and distorted.
My armour is hidden, lightweight, but protective: Frodo's mithril vest.
My torso is solid.
I tap gleeful drumbeats on my front with my hands,
remembering how the boys used to do this on their own chests in marching band.
I would not survive a jousting match; but I no longer need to compete.

Senseless

Wafting cologne means my parents are going out for the night.
I will miss them.
I wander in and out of their room.
I am seven years old, or maybe a teenager.
Now the memory blurs: the smell absent and living with my family happened so long ago.
Sometimes I forget what it's like to be close to people.

Life sentences

I am imprisoned in that jail cell again,
locked in with only my punishing thoughts for company.
Dank regrets and failures drip from the walls.
There's no use pounding on the door as no one can hear me in this subterranean dead zone.
And what's there to say anyway?
I was the one who locked myself in here and tossed the keys in the Thames,
ensuring a chosen life sentence, or worse.
Traitors' Gate: its barbarous heritage perfect for my wrongdoings; medieval punishment the only proportionate justice.
No trial needed, I beseech the hangman, I am irredeemable.
Rats and plague crawl around my bare feet.
I am no better than the disintegrating bones of previous occupants, and my feverish decline might end me before I even get to the noose.

I've just come home from an autumnal run, leaving the bar door open behind me.
There is time for a hot shower, then a coffee.
The guilt has been managed this morning, after all.
Standing on the balcony I look towards the river and that slimy cell.
No punishment today, my poor Polly head.
Put it into sentences.
I pull on my favourite woollen jumper, open my laptop,
fingertips to keys, and set myself free.

Inside outside

The family in the dusty framed photo, enlarged and bulbous with a blue tint, is seen through the water bottle as you drink.

The wind whipping against the seized up, shuddering wooden sash window reminds you of being in a caravan at North Morte Farm.

A single seagull lands suspiciously on the tall streetlight, eye level to your view, looks around sceptically, and flies.

From below, arguments and giggles, screeches and swear words emanate, disembodied. Coming and going, the sounds are fleeting, breaking waves at the seashore, some ferocious, some meek.

The sirens fill the air from time to time, echoing against the buildings, azure lights flashing, reminding you of all the danger. But rather than lure you in, like their ancient predecessors, you pause, take note, momentarily aware.

Falling awake

Daylight falls on the bed.
Eyelashes scrape the pillow.
My body stretches and says thanks.
I thank my legs, torso, arms, face. We are whole.
I sink down, swimming in the duvet and sheet caresses,
unfurling myself.
Warmth cradles my skin, free from pyjamas.
Clouds are on vacation and the blue spreads out, slathered on,
buttering the heavens, as seagulls surf.
Disappearing into this morning's embrace, this melting moment,
absorbed completely, I am sponged up in brightness.
The sun has woken up.

Bedsit belongings

All the best things in here were gifts.
My hanging spider plant keeps me company and I can be reclusive.
My indoor bistro table houses a few letters, from the bank and my pension fund, rather than a cappuccino and an ashtray.
The Woolacombe tea towel is used for drying up,
and I am a stickler for routine.
I am in love with the pictures on the wall. Picasso.
Medication lives in a plastic sandwich Tupperware, red with a floral pattern.
I miss yelling things up and down stairs at family.
A portable, waterproof Bluetooth speaker represents the extent of my hi-fi capabilities.
A candle, there by the lamp, is lit when I'm feeling extravagant and cosy.
I am proud of my minimalist lifestyle, though I horde black socks.
'I'm ready to be kissed,' I used to yell from my bedroom before sleep every night.
My family photo frames are all here now, rescued from the dark days of the dumpster.
Mundane things give me pleasure: orange squash.
The submarine grey linoleum flooring by the kitchenette is styled to look metallic.
Some thought went into this design, humble but practical.
I yearn for the sound of other people coming home.

Blood ants

“Life loves to be taken by the lapel and told: I’m with you kid. Let’s go.” —Maya Angelou

So, this is life?
I’m so far from Alton Infants School and micromachine loves.
My best friend Stuart I had to say goodbye to.
Now there are blood ants in the playground where I have to be.
My first six years are completely taken.
I’m 33.8711° N, 117.8628° W with new rules to live by:
I pledge allegiance to the…
brainwashing: the red ribbon with a new meaning on my lapel.
There is no option not to say the pledge and
I always do what I’m told.
The heat, the constant putrid milk, the earthquake blacktop: I’m
sickened by the paste, dirty from fingers, that I have to work with.
No one is listening or saying, ‘I’m here for you.’
I am barely even a kid.
I shorten my a’s and turn my t’s into d’s, but let’s
not forget: some make America home — I didn’t want to go.

Guernica

I am the bull.
My lopsided eyes and prominent ear are contorted; the anguish of a dying clown's smudged makeup.
I am in as much turmoil as the rest of us, twisted, test case collateral damage death.
My natural strength has been violently neutralised and I've the power of a lab rat.
I am here on the side where I smell carcasses burning.
To my left, I notice the horse is dying faster than I am.
Once of use, we will soon be remains.
But what of this lightbulb?
It shines, the sun, yellow, above my head and the other heads.
It reveals something new now: you.
You!
The Polly sharing an apartment in LA in 2006.
You like your history, but this is too much, sticking us to the wall, a mere aspect of interior design.
What do you want from us?
You wake every day staring at us from your pillow, as we perish anew with each of your palm tree sunrises.
You are perverse in the voyeurism of our demise.
And your interpretation is unfounded.
The last supper?
No way.
We are merely life being destroyed.

Unkind flowers

You sat on that couch.
Beautiful, you wore the kimono.
You loved me softly, I remember.
You were unkind and tigerish when I told you I felt sad.

Hair is everything

Trudging the inhospitable terrain of pores,
I notice them sprouting.
Thrash, I must thrash them, the upshoots,
with pink polymer Barbie blades.
It's normal to bleed.

Voiding vegetation from at least upper shins down is tough work:
clearing the bush,
taming it for the tourists.

Dreaming of unapologetic locks, lush topography, wild and unploughed,
a tiny landscape of rivulets and forests between knee joint and foot,
I imagine what could be and toss the razor.

Ode to a coconut

Oh, you perplexing hedgehog.
I love you like sand between toes and in ears after all day beach.
I find you rough, like cracked heels, but adorable.
My darling sandpaper planet, you are orbiting the fruit bowl
because I have no idea what to do with you.
You are a lonely hut on the Yorkshire moors: hard to reach; a
novel inside.
Dearest coconut, sometimes you are Britain, sometimes you are as
Californian as a lifeguard tower, advising fragrant piña colada
Banana Boat sunscreen on an already-burnt face.
So different outside from in, you are solid wood filled with waves.
I shake you and I am diving into the sea.
Offering freedom, you are somehow also unyielding.
My knee aches still, scraped-up from that fall on brown beams,
and I know you could hurt me just the same.
But love, you are deceptively sensitive, born of sun, dryness and
hydration,
the very best contradiction.
Pretending to be impenetrable, you are life itself.
I envy your protective uniform.
I am inside out.
You are too wise to make that mistake.

Recording

The little rubber monkey sits politely on the arm, pushing the needle into the grooves.
Grandpa hums along as Granny taps her foot to the syncopation.
I write in my journal, articulating the pages with drawings.
We went to Knole Park today.
We went to the Bucks Head today.
Tomorrow we will go to Hastings.
Tomorrow we will listen to another record.
Until we won't. And we don't. And they don't.

Turn back into water

Seven minutes: the time it takes a raindrop to hit the earth.
We barely know our own fallen minds; in fact, we don't.
I don't know mine, yet even a cloud knows it's time to burst.
We have now.
Sure.
We always have now,
like the half-finished, lukewarm cup of decaf, initially promising,
but now a liquid burden.
And in this now we are complicated.
Little more than yesterday, and little less than tomorrow.
We must be.
The drop of water tips from one side of the penny in a statement
unfathomable.
When it lands it is either soaked up quickly in the smoke-scented
green carpet, or slowly, by degrees, with the air.
We are this droplet.
And that time I dripped tears at the New Year's Eve party only
existed that night. The tsunami destroyed, but the reality stayed in
the past.
The reality stayed in the past.
Because the perishing moment by moment transforms us.
And we join our fellow molecules regardless.
We are just this.
Shape changes.
We have at least three states and all the transitions in between.
We breathe a sigh of relief, temporary of course.
Rivers run their course in hundreds of years and then go.
They go.
And new ones pour from new sources according to new forces
that we do not control.
We are all this: running and freezing and steaming; I will stop
scheming.
We are moving.
We have seven minutes to turn to water, before we crash land.

Kings Cross 2.0

Spit with strength at the shape-shift station.
We are wiping away muck with no placation.
Sweep, sweep, sweep the imperfects away.
There is a gold-tied man with his gold-drenched display.

Set fire to the dustbins, set fire to the bedraggled.
Kick the stench up the road where the marketeers haggled.
Close your eyes to the death storm, don't look left or right.
We don't want any humans here, only robotic delight.

And who cares anyway if a heathen shatters.
Who cares at all, as if any of now matters.
We must aspire to copper lampshades, this is all I know.
In their treacle illumination, we'll forget the long ago.

Pigeon spotting

I lie on my belly so as not to scare you,
a slowworm, slithering forward and peering.
We are six days in.

You are ravenous,
eking out life from another mouth.
I am not dangerous behind the glass,
but I am besotted, of course.

Determined furry custards,
each no bigger than a ramekin,
a mere pudding for a bigger bird.

Surge up your muscles, you dollops of wings, beaks and feet.
Face your fates.
The jet stream will see you soar.
A hopeless Icarus, I am left behind, staring in envy.

Olive Sabina Gifford Bull

'I wish my name were Sabina,' she used to always say.
She randomly used versions of her name on different forms, infuriating Dad.
Sabina wrote poetry on a loud, clackety typewriter and entered competitions.
She won a jet-ski and a holiday in Nice, after writing a poem about David Hasselhoff.
My parents were gifted these awards as she had no use for either.
Sabina wrote stories that I never read.
Where she lived with Grandpa in Birmingham was always cold and the kitchen smelled of the gas oven, but the house was detached and they were proud.
We didn't mind the cold because we lived in California.
The bathtub was olive green and breakfast was Mars chocolate bars, cut up in bowls.
'Bread and water for tea,' she would threaten if we misbehaved.
She never followed through and we loved the occasion of a custard tart. Pineapple juice.
Her skin was pale and soft as butter, having avoided all sun.
Grandma read tarot cards, palms, astrology and the number of wrinkles on our wrists.
She broke her nose in a lights-out air raid, fear her greatest enemy.
Grandma had to leave school at fourteen to look after her siblings.
Sabina was a writer and a poet.
Nothing survives of her writing.
I wish my name were Sabina.

Footsteps from above

Our planet has crystallised and I'm inside, deep beneath the surface.
Sitting cross-legged, I knead the fleshy arch of my bare foot with both hands.
I wonder about everyone else's feet, their impact on the transparent ground above.
Shapes, sizes, the cadence when walking or running.
Or their absence: the feet are broken or simply gone.
Inside Earth, from Moria, I hear their determined steps pounding above.
Greyish footprints visible on the surface, bare or booted, falling heavily, lightly, unstoppable.
I feel the ballet dancer's pirouettes, the storming of the Bastille, the blue pogo stick kid bouncing, and the springy gymnast hurtling through air, landing neatly, both feet flushed together, as pilgrims' hands do touch.
I know nothing of the feet owners, but this relentless treading is beautiful.
Marching.
Stamping.
Striding united.
From within our planet's heart, it is clear: these feet are all equal.

www.ingramcontent.com/pod-product-compliance
Ingram Content Group UK Ltd.
Pitfield, Milton Keynes, MK11 3LW, UK
UKHW021036270726
13967UKWH00013B/2662